Heroes or Villains?

Contents

Haydn Middleton

OXFORD

Introduction

Have you ever seen a TV programme or film where a person is 'on trial'? The person has been accused of committing a crime. Did the accused really do it, though?
Is he or she **guilty** or **innocent?**

The people who decide are the **judge** and the **jury**. They hope to give the right decision (or **verdict**) but first they need to hear a lot of information about the crime. To get this information, they listen to what two **lawyers** tell them.

The judge and jury listens to each side of the story.

One lawyer tells the judge and jury how and why the accused *did* commit the crime. The other lawyer tells them that the accused couldn't *possibly* have done it. Both lawyers are talking about exactly the same crime and exactly the same person but their stories can be very different. It depends on which facts they use as **evidence**. Sometimes, they look at the *same* facts in very different ways!

The judge and jury have to decide which side they believe.

Then they give their verdict:

INNOCENT
OR
GUILTY?

Two sides to every story

There are two sides to most stories. Very little in real life is either all good or all bad.

Look at someone you know very well: you! You've done lots of things you're really proud of, right? Like helping people. Have you never *ever* told a little white lie or been mean? You see – the same person, two different ways of behaving!

There's a bit of the villain in every hero. Even Spiderman shows his dark side in *Spiderman 3!*

The **media** can make famous people seem both good *and* bad. Some reports make them sound like heroes or heroines while others make them sound like villains.

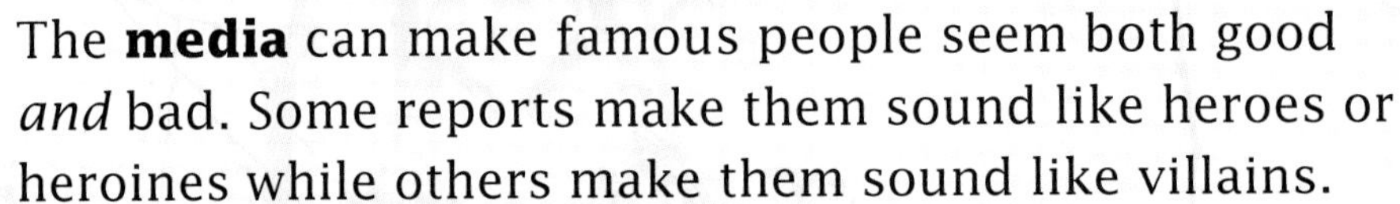

The
BUGLE
SPIDERMAN:
OUR HERO

The
DAILY ECHO
SPIDEY
THE SCOUNDREL

You might ask yourself "How can this be?" The facts must *prove* they are one thing or the other? Well, do they? Let's take a look at someone from hundreds of years ago ...

Robin Hood: saint or sinner?

Robin Hood is a famous character from legend. He was said to live with a band of followers in Sherwood Forest, near Nottingham, in the middle of England.

Robin Hood and his merry men.

Robin Hood's mission in life was to take from the rich and give to the poor. That sounds like a good thing. It makes Robin a hero, right?

Well, if you were a poor person, yes he was. If Robin gave you money or food, you would think he was a hero.

What if you were a rich person, though? What if Robin stole your precious belongings and simply gave them away? You would want to get the Sheriff of Nottingham on to him, fast!

So Robin Hood was either a hero or a villain. It all depended on whose side of the story you agreed with.

Robin Hood may not have existed except in stories but the media today treats people as heroes *and* villains.

In this book we'll look at some real life famous people:

- a footballer (see page 8)
- a businessman (see page 12)
- a climber (see page 16)
- a sculptor (see page 20)
- a racing-car driver (see page 24).

First we'll see *why* there are two sides to each person's story. Then it's up to you to give *your* verdict – hero or villain.

Zinedine Zidane: a national hero

Zidane: the facts

- Clubs: Cannes (France), Bordeaux (France), Juventus (Italy), Real Madrid (Spain)
- World Player of the Year: 1998, 2000, 2003
- World Cup Winner 1998
- Voted 'Best European Player of the Past 50 Years' 2004
- Voted 'Most Outstanding Player' of World Cup Finals 2006
- World Record Transfer Fee (66 million US dollars) paid for him in 2001

Zinedine Zidane is one of the all-time great footballers. In 1998 he scored two goals to help win the World Cup Final for France. Eight years later he was back in the World Cup Final as captain of his country. There he hit another goal in his last game before he retired. Only four players in history have scored in two different World Cup Finals!

Beauty on the ball

Zidane wasn't just a winner. He was a beautiful player to watch. He grew up in a poor, tough neighbourhood in France but he played football as if he had superhuman skills.

"When we don't know what to do," one of his French teammates once said, "we just give the ball to Zidane and he works something out." No true football fan will ever forget Zidane. In France they even wanted to make him President!

Zidane's image is beamed onto the Arc de Triomphe in Paris after the 1998 World Cup victory.

Yet there is another side to the Zinedine Zidane story...

Zidane: a national disgrace

Zinedine Zidane could play football. Make no mistake about that. But he will not be remembered only for his talent. He will also be remembered for his anger. For while Zidane could control a football, he could not control his own temper.

He was sent off *14 times* in his career. Even in 1998, on the way to winning the World Cup, he was sent off for stamping on a Saudi Arabian player. Finally, he was sent off in the 2006 World Cup Final for head-butting Marco Materazzi of Italy. Can such a violent sportsman be called an all-time great?

Zidane is shown the red card and sent off in the 2006 World Cup Final.

Some say that badly behaved footballers set a poor example to their fans.

Beauty and the beast

People say other players provoked Zidane too much. Maybe opponents did say vile things to him but shouldn't true heroes ignore such abuse? With only ten men left on the field, France lost the 2006 World Cup Final. Zidane let everyone down that day – himself, his team, his fans, his sport and his country. Can we look back and admire his beauty as a player, when he also behaved like such a beast?

So what's *your* verdict?

Can a sports star play dirty and still be a hero?

Good guy Gates

QUESTION: So you're a big fan of Bill Gates?

ANSWER: What's not to like? With his company Microsoft® he's given us brilliant, easy-to-use computer software. What a gift! Computers used to be big and slow and hard to operate. There were no images and icons, just lines and lines of text. Now, thanks to Bill, nearly everyone's got a cool little PC.

QUESTION: Do all computers use his software?

ANSWER: Not quite all. Most computers come with Microsoft® software already installed. Businessman Bill's made sure of that! His software is so reliable and so simple. As I said – a real gift to the human race.

Bill Gates designed software that changed the face of computing.

http://www.haveyoursay.px

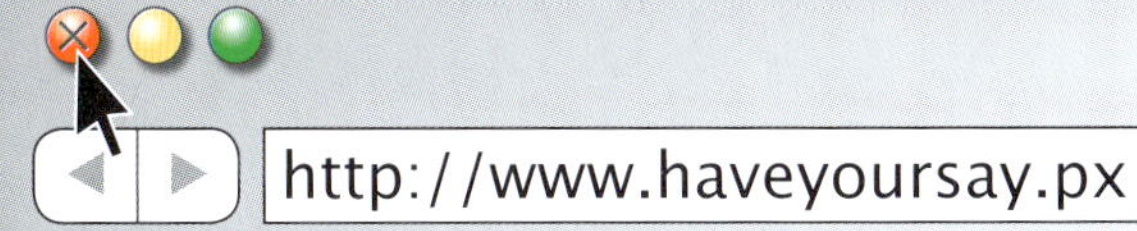

QUESTION: He must be a very successful businessman. Has he made a lot of money?

ANSWER: He's one of the richest people in the world. He's *also* the most generous guy in history.

QUESTION: Who is he generous to?

ANSWER: To charities. His money helps to sort out health and education problems, especially in poor countries. By the time he dies, he plans to give nearly all his money away. So no, he's not just a businessman. If he didn't already have everything he wanted, I'd give him a gift back!

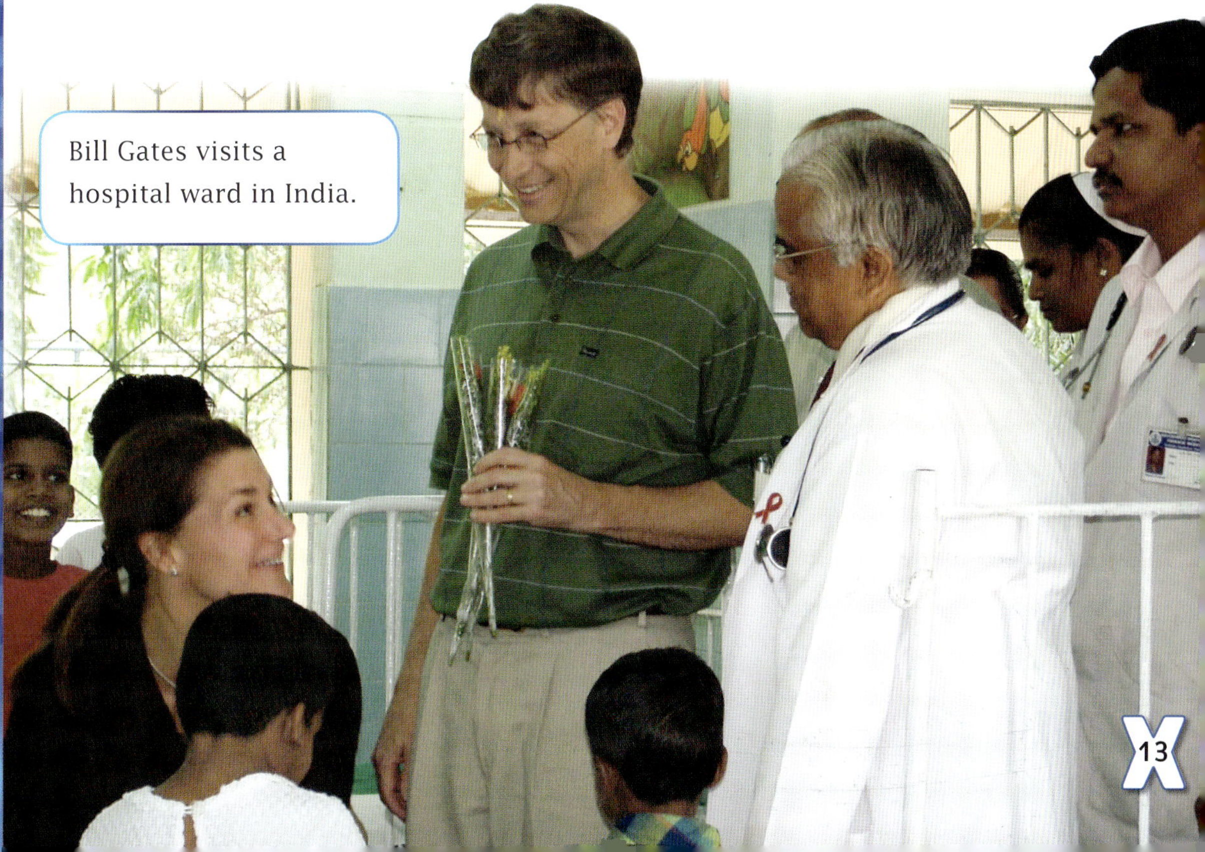

Bill Gates visits a hospital ward in India.

Bad guy Bill

QUESTION: So you're not such a Bill Gates fan?

ANSWER: No way! He's bad news for the computer world.

QUESTION: Doesn't Microsoft® make good products?

ANSWER: Sure, but other companies do too and Gates stands in their way. It's unhealthy. Other companies might make better products – but no one would know. Gates stops computer users having a real choice. It's sort of against the law.

QUESTION: So why don't people take him to court?

ANSWER: They do. Gates has had to pay some huge **fines**.

QUESTION: Why hasn't that stopped him?

ANSWER: Because fines don't make a difference to such a rich man. He can afford to pay them.

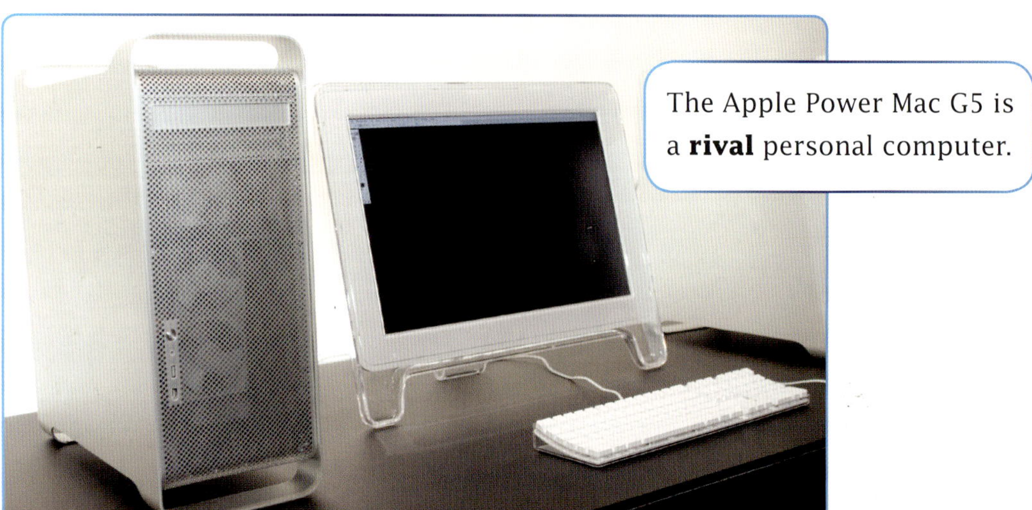

The Apple Power Mac G5 is a **rival** personal computer.

http://www.haveyoursay.px

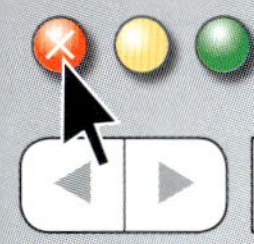

QUESTION: He's generous to charities, isn't he?

ANSWER: Yes – but even that helps him get more customers. Giving money to poor countries is a good way to influence their governments and get his products even more established there. Boy, does he let everyone *know* how generous he is. It's great free publicity!

In 2005, Bill Gates was made a knight by the Queen for his **services** to business and charity work.

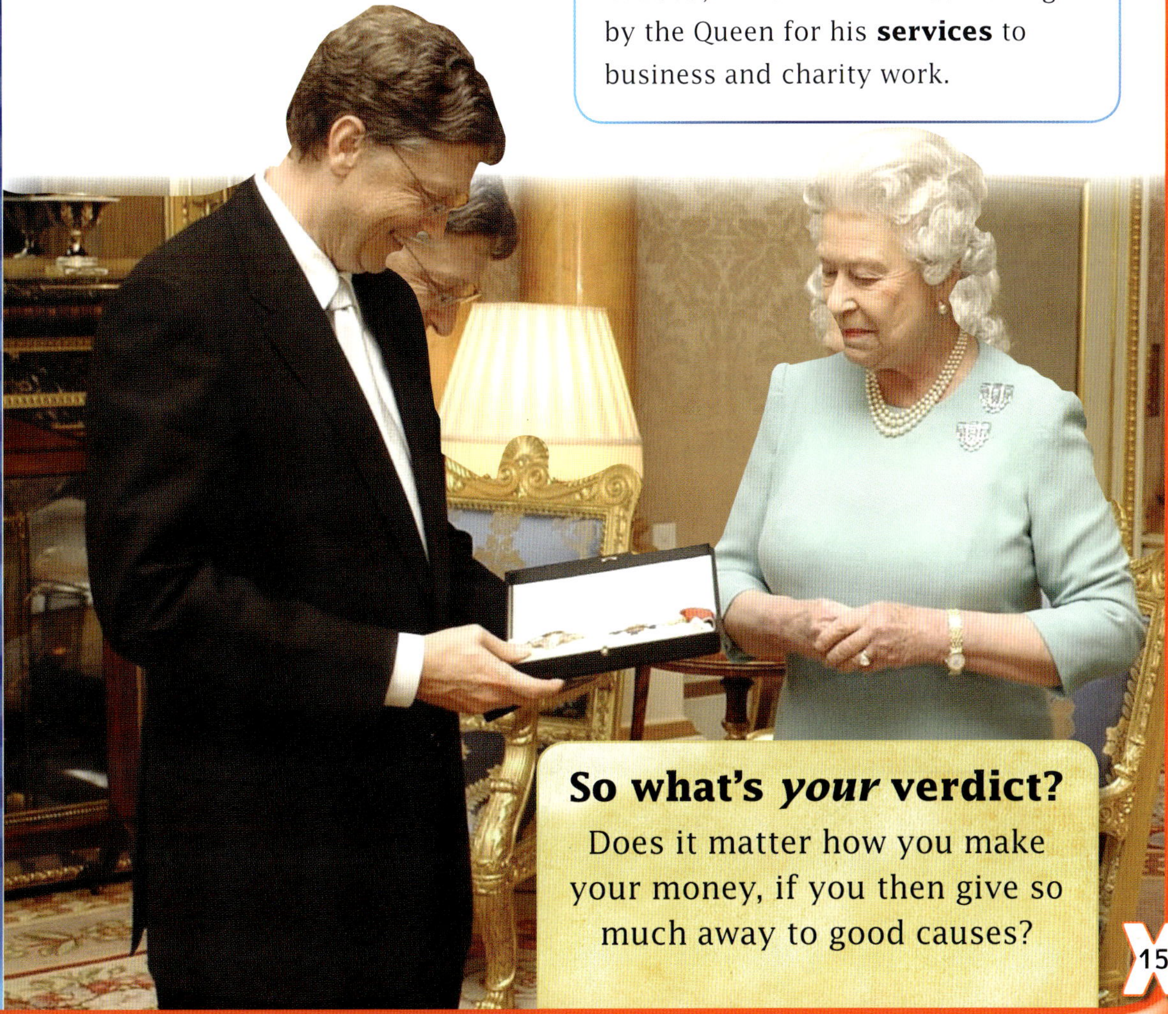

So what's *your* verdict?

Does it matter how you make your money, if you then give so much away to good causes?

Top of the world!

When Alison Hargreaves was a girl growing up in Britain, not many women climbed the world's highest mountains. Climbing was what men did or that's what most people thought. Alison didn't think that way.

By the age of 33, Alison was one of the world's top mountain climbers and also one of the most famous. She was not much more than one and a half metres tall but she was brave and fit and strong. She climbed the incredibly dangerous North Face of the Eiger in the Alps – when she was pregnant!

Three in a row

In 1995, Alison set herself a tough new challenge. She decided to climb the world's three highest mountains, one after the other. She reached the top of the very highest mountain, Mount Everest, without oxygen or any help from **sherpas**.

Soon afterwards, she made it to the summit of the next highest mountain, K2 in Pakistan. Then a violent storm broke out. Alison never came down that mountain. Her body was never found. Everyone **mourned** a true heroine. Well, not *quite* everyone ...

Alison reached the top of mount Everest, the highest mountain.

Alison and her children climbed together.

Fame or family?

Star Letter

Dear Editor

Alison Hargreaves was a talented climber. Anyone could see that. When you have such a talent you have to go with it but as a wife and mother, Alison had other responsibilities too. Did she really have to make such dangerous climbs? Did she have to dice with death – then leave her poor children motherless at the ages of six and four? Surely a mother's true place is in the home.

Australian TV wildlife expert, Steve Irwin, mixed with dangerous creatures for a living. In 2006, he was killed by a stingray. Like Alison, Steve had two young children.

Star Letter

Dear Editor

Do people ever say *fathers* shouldn't take risks? Do dads who climb mountains or drive racing cars get blamed for not being there for their children? Steve Irwin worked with dangerous animals. Did people say he shouldn't take risks because of his children? One way or another, life is always about taking risks – for women and men.

So what's *your* verdict?

Should mothers and fathers be more careful about the risks they take? Or should they live their lives how they want to?

Man in the landscape

Here are two reviews from *Arts Review* about Antony Gormley's sculptures.

Arts Review
2005

ANOTHER PLACE

Another Place is a show by Britain's famous sculptor, Antony Gormley. His hundred metal men do not stand in a **studio** or gallery. They are fixed to Crosby Beach in northern England.

The men are all models of Gormley's own body. The tide comes in and out but it never sweeps them away. They are spooky, sad, proud and strong.

You can walk among them, touch them, think about them. They can *mean* whatever you want them to mean. That is their beauty.

Another Place by Antony Gormley.

EVENT HORIZON

In a 2007 exhibition called *Event Horizon*, 30 more of Gormley's metal men stand on London's skyline. They make us look up, when so often we just look down. They make us think about our own place in the built-up city and about how we relate to each other. "It's amazing what happens," says Gormley, "when the world itself becomes the studio." He is a twenty-first-century genius, making us ask where human beings belong today.

One of the 30 rooftop figures that make up *Event Horizon* by Antony Gormley.

One man everywhere

Here's a very different view of Antony Gormley's work.

Art News, 2007

Antony Gormley's been at it again. Sticking his blank-faced metal men all over our beaches and cities. So what's new? See one of his sculptures and you've seen the lot – because they are all just images of him!

Why does he want to see himself everywhere? He must be a real show-off! Gormley doesn't even carve out his own statues. He gets other people to take casts of his body. As the art critic Brian Sewell put it, "He has absolutely no artistic merit".

There's a safety problem with his work too. Thirty-three million motorists a year drive past his monstrous *Angel of the North* in northern England. Their eyes are meant to be on the road. Instead, they end up looking at the giant statue. It could cause road accidents.

Antony Gormley's 20 metre high sculpture *Angel of the North*, 1998.

When the tide is in on Crosby Beach, boats could smash into his metal men. Even visitors to that show could be swept out to sea.

Wise up, Mr G. The genius sculptors of the past created proper art for galleries, not just copies of themselves. It's really not all about *you*.

Winning in style

When it comes to Formula One motor racing, the **statistics** don't lie. Since the championship began in 1950, 28 different drivers have won the title. Fourteen have won it more than once. One man has won it seven times.

That man is Michael Schumacher, from Germany. He was the finest racing-driver the world has ever seen.

Schumacher also recorded:
- most race victories (91)
- most wins in a season (13)
- most points scored in a season (148)
- most consecutive days as world champion (1813 days: from 8 October, 2000 to 25 September, 2005).

Hail to the 'Rain King'

Schumacher kept himself amazingly fit for the teams
he raced for – first Jordan, then Benetton, then Ferrari.
Physically fit *and* mentally fit. He could make split-second
decisions at awesome speeds, even in high-risk wet weather
conditions. That's why people called him the Rain King.

Schumacher was well rewarded
for his success on the track.
He became the world's first
billionaire sportsperson.
He didn't spend it all on
himself either. After the
Asian Tsunami disaster
of 2004, he made a
personal donation of
10 million US dollars to
help the victims.

Winning ugly

Michael Schumacher knew how to win races. He also knew how to stop other drivers winning. In doing that, he didn't always stick to the rules. Three **incidents** show this.

Australia 1994

The Australian Grand Prix was the last race of the Formula One **season**. Schumacher was just one point ahead of Damon Hill in the World Championship. Schumacher collided with Hill's car, putting them both out of the race. This meant neither driver could score any points that day, so Schumacher won the championship.

Michael Schumacher (right) crashes into Damon Hill (left) putting Hill out of the running for the 1994 title.

Monaco 2006

At the Monaco Grand Prix when his rival Fernando Alonso tried to beat his qualifying time, Schumacher crashed into Alonso's car. He blocked a part of the **circuit** meaning Alonso had to slow down.

Spain 1997

At the Spanish Grand Prix Michael Schumacher was again just one point ahead of his main rival, Jacques Villeneuve. During the race he tried to ram Villeneuve's car. As a result, he was disqualified from the whole championship that year.

Are these the actions of a true champion or more like the actions of a cheat?

Michael Schumacher (left) rams into Jacques Villeneuve (right).

So what's *your* verdict?

Does a true champion have to win at all costs?

Thinking for yourself

So now you have read about the footballer, the businessman, the climber, the sculptor and the racing car driver. How did they seem to you: like heroes or like villains?

Did you notice than in each case, the 'good' side of the story came first? Then you read the 'bad' side. When people become famous – for whatever reason – the media often treats them that way. First it writes positive stories about the person, then it starts to **criticize**.

10 HEROIC LIONS ONE STUPID BOY

NGLAND goalscorer Michael Owen weeps on a team-mate's shoulders after our brave lions' tragic World Cup defeat on penalties against Argentina last night. Glenn Hoddle's team fought he heroes after being reduced to 10 men early in the second half because of David Beckham's stupid sending off for aiming a kick at an opposition player. Now he must be kicking himself...

END OF ENGLAND'S DREAM - PAGES 2,3,4,5 AND SPORT

Some famous people are criticised *because* they are famous. This is because people who succeed in life stand out.

Sometimes the media even make up stories and **scandals** about famous people, just to sell their newspaper or magazine. So you can't always believe everything you read!

There are two sides to every story. Like lawyers in a courtroom, **journalists** can present the same facts in very different ways.

Your own verdict

We need the media to tell us about stars like Zinedine Zidane and Michael Schumacher but we don't need to believe everything we read or see on TV. Often the media is just giving an *opinion* on a person.

What we really need to know are the *facts*. Then we can give our *own* verdicts.

As you have seen in this book, there are two sides to most people's stories.

Your friends aren't purely good or bad. Nor are most famous people. Gather information about them, not just opinions. Then you will probably decide they are just like most human beings – not total heroes, not total villains, just a bit of both!

Glossary

circuit	a race track
criticize	to say what you do not like about something
evidence	anything used to show that something is true or that something happened
fine	money someone has to pay as punishment
guilty	to have done something wrong
incident	something that happens, especially something unusual or unpleasant
innocent	not guilty
journalist	a person who writes for a newspaper or presents the news on the television or radio
judge	a person who runs a trial
jury	a group of people who decide if someone accused of a crime is guilty
lawyer	a person who is trained to advise people about the law and to represent them in a court of law
media	the television, radio, internet and newspapers
mourn	to be sad because someone has died
rival	someone competing with you
scandal	unkind talk about someone who is supposed to have done something wrong
season	the length of time in a competition
service	something that is done to help people
Sherpas	people who live in the Himalayan mountains
statistics	information recorded as numbers
studio	a place where an artist works
verdict	a decision in a court of law or when something has been tested or considered carefully

Index

Why not read these two great stories about heroes and villains?

Jake Jones v Vlad the Bad

Air Scare